D1219502

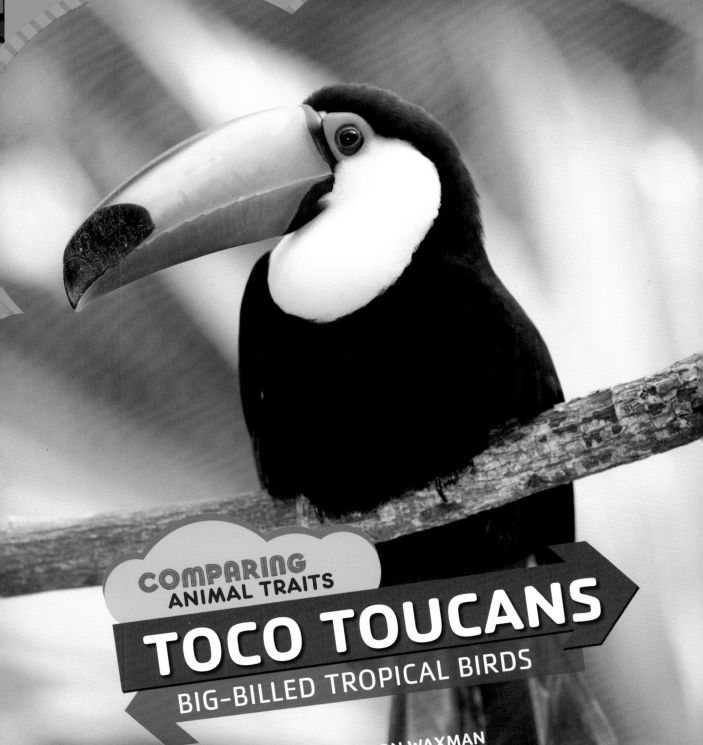

COMPARING ANIMAL TRAITS

# TOCO TOUCANS
## BIG-BILLED TROPICAL BIRDS

LAURA HAMILTON WAXMAN

Lerner Publications ◆ Minneapolis

*For Yana, my lovable bird lover*

Lerner Publications Company
A division of Lerner Publishing Group, Inc.
241 First Avenue North
Minneapolis, MN 55401 USA

For reading levels and more information, look up this title at www.lernerbooks.com.


Photo Acknowledgments

The images in this book are used with the permission of: © iStockphoto.com/edurivero, p. 1; © Panoramic Images/Getty Images, p. 4; © iStockphoto.com/JackF, p. 5; © iStockphoto.com/Global_Pics, p. 6; © iStockphoto.com/scanrail, p. 7; © iStockphoto.com/Detanan, p. 8 (left), 11, 17 (left); © Frans Lanting/Mint Images/Getty Images, p. 8 (right); © iStockphoto.com/pchoui, p. 9 (top); © Moment Open/Getty Images, p. 9 (bottom); © Roberta Olenick/All Canada Photos/Getty Images, p. 10; © Alan Murphy/Minden Pictures/ Getty Images, p. 11 (right), 14; © Laura Westlund/Independent Picture Service, p. 12; © Steve Winter/ National Geographic/Getty Images, p. 13 (top); © Colombini Medeiros, Fabio/Animals Animals/Earth Scenes, p. 13 (bottom); © Pete Oxford/Minden Pictures/CORBIS, p. 15; © Altrendo Nature/Getty Images, p. 16; © Glenn Bartley/Minden Pictures/Getty Images, p. 17 (right); © Nature Picture Library/Alamy, p. 18; © Panoramic Images/Getty Images, p. 19 (top); © Luiz Antonio da Silva/Shutterstock.com, p. 19 (bottom); © Kichigin/Shutterstock.com, p. 20; © LorraineHudgins/Shutterstock.com, p. 21; © Michael Crowley/ Moment/Getty Images, p. 22; © Brian Lasenby/Shutterstock.com, p. 23 (right); Haroldo Pablo Jr/NHPA/ Photoshot/Newscom, pp. 23 (left), 25; © Art Wolfe/Getty Images, p. 24; © Jim Zipp/Science Source/Getty Images, p. 26; © Marigo, Luiz Claudio / Animals Animals/Earth Scenes, p. 27 (left); © Gary Mszaros/Getty Images, p. 27 (right); © Image Source/Getty Images, p. 28; © Martin Harvey/Getty Images, p. 29.

Front cover: © iStockphoto.com/Denja1.
Back cover: © Luiz C. Ribeiro/Shutterstock.com.


Main body text set in Calvert MT Std 12/18. Typeface provided by Monotype Typography.


**Library of Congress Cataloging-in-Publication Data**

Waxman, Laura Hamilton, author.
    Toco toucans : big-billed tropical birds / Laura Hamilton Waxman.
        pages cm. — (Comparing animal traits)
    Audience: Ages 7–10.
    Audience: K to grade 3.
    Includes bibliographical references.
    ISBN 978-1-4677-9510-4 (lb : alk. paper) — ISBN 978-1-4677-9635-4 (pb : alk. paper) —
ISBN 978-1-4677-9636-1 (eb pdf)
    1. Toucans—Juvenile literature.  I. Title.
QL696.P57W39  2016
598.7'2—dc23                                          2015017439

Manufactured in the United States of America
1 – BP – 12/31/15

# TABLE OF CONTENTS

Introduction
**MEET THE TOCO TOUCAN** .................................................. 4

Chapter 1
**WHAT DO TOCO TOUCANS LOOK LIKE?** .............. 6

Chapter 2
**WHERE DO TOCO TOUCANS LIVE?** ................... 12

Chapter 3
**TOCO TOUCANS IN ACTION** ............................. 18

Chapter 4
**THE LIFE CYCLE OF A TOCO TOUCAN** .............. 24

Toco Toucan Trait Chart          30
Glossary                         31
Selected Bibliography            32
Further Information              32
Index                            32

# MEET THE TOCO TOUCAN

**A toco toucan hops from branch to branch at the edge of a tropical forest.** Toco toucans are a kind of bird. Other kinds of animals you might know are insects, reptiles, amphibians, mammals, and fish.

Toco toucans can fly for only short distances.

All birds share common traits. For example, they are all warm-blooded. That means they make their own body heat and keep a steady temperature. All birds are vertebrates, or animals with backbones. They all have a beak and feathers and lay hard-shelled eggs. Toco toucans share these traits with other birds. But some features set this bird apart.

# CHAPTER 1

# WHAT DO TOCO TOUCANS LOOK LIKE?

**Toco toucans are the largest of all toucan** species**.** They weigh about 1.5 pounds (0.7 kilograms). They have a large bill that makes up one-third of their length. From bill to tail, they measure about 2 feet (0.6 meters).

The reddish-orange bill of a toco toucan is lightweight. That's because it is made of foamlike bone with many air pockets. The bill is protected by a hard outer shell of keratin. This is the same strong material that's in human fingernails.

**DID YOU KNOW?**
There are about **FORTY** species of toucans in the world.

Toco toucans are covered with glossy black feathers. White feathers cover their throat and upper chest. They have long white and black tail feathers. They hop from tree to tree or fly short distances with their short, wide wings.

# TOCO TOUCANS VS. KEEL-BILLED TOUCANS

A keel-billed toucan hops from branch to branch searching for fruit to eat. Keel-billed toucans live inside the dense tropical forests of South America. They look a lot like toco toucans but are slightly smaller. They weigh less than a pound (0.5 kg). They have bright yellow feathers on their head and chest.

Like the toco toucan, the keel-billed toucan has a very large bill. The bill of the keel-billed toucan, though, is more colorful. The bill of both birds camouflages them against the brightly colored fruits and flowers around them.

The toco toucan (*left*) has a mostly orange beak, while the keel-billed toucan has a mostly green beak.

Like the toco toucan, the keel-billed toucan has strong legs and feet.

The feet of toco toucans and keel-billed toucans are also the same. Two toes point forward, and two point backward. This foot shape helps the birds perch, climb, and hop. Both birds have short wings and long tail feathers. These traits make both the toco toucan and the keel-billed toucan good gliders but clumsy long-distance fliers.

**DID YOU KNOW?**
A toucan's bill helps the bird **COOL DOWN** in hot weather. The bill gives off body heat. The hotter the toucan gets, the more heat the bill releases.

# TOCO TOUCANS VS. NORTHERN BOBWHITES

A northern bobwhite pecks at the ground. *Crunch!* It cracks a seed in its hard, black beak. Northern bobwhites are small, pudgy birds. They measure about 10 inches (25 centimeters) from beak to tail. At about 6 ounces (170 grams), they weigh much less than toucans.

Unlike toucans, northern bobwhites have a round body. They have a small head and a small, cone-shaped beak. Their wings are rounded, and their tail feathers are short.

Northern bobwhites are mostly brown. Their color blends in with the ground, where they spend most of their time. Their feet and claws are suited for scratching in the dirt to find seeds. Northern bobwhites have three toes pointing forward and one shorter toe pointing backward.

A young northern bobwhite drinks from a pond.

# COMPARE IT!

**TOCO TOUCANS**

VS.

**NORTHERN BOBWHITES**

**24 INCHES** (61 CM)   ◄ AVERAGE LENGTH ►   **10 INCHES** (25 CM)

**LARGE AND CURVED**   ◄ BILL ►   **SMALL AND CONE-SHAPED**

Yes   ◄ LONG TAIL FEATHERS? ►   No

# CHAPTER 2

# WHERE DO TOCO TOUCANS LIVE?

**Toco toucans are tropical birds of South America.** Their habitat includes tropical forests or grassy plains called savannas. They live near streams or ponds for drinking water.

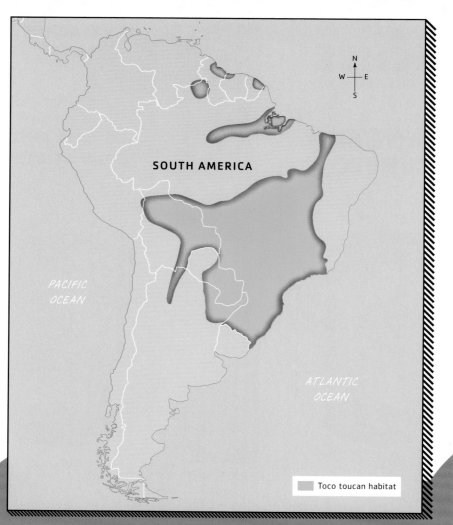

N
W · E
S

SOUTH AMERICA

PACIFIC
OCEAN

ATLANTIC
OCEAN

Toco toucan habitat

The top layer of trees where the toucan lives is called the canopy.

Toco toucans rely on the trees in their habitat for the tropical fruits they eat. They spend a lot of time in the top branches of trees. This is where toco toucans find ripe fruit. They also depend on the trees of their habitat for shelter. Toco toucans often **roost** in natural holes in trees, sometimes sharing a hole with up to four other toucans.

### DID YOU KNOW?

To fit inside a roosting hole, toco toucans form into a **TIGHT BALL**. First, they turn their head around and rest their bill on their back. Then they fold their tail up over their head.

# TOCO TOUCANS VS. TROPICAL KINGBIRDS

*Pip-pip-pip-pip.* A tropical kingbird sings from its low perch in a tree. Like toco toucans, tropical kingbirds seek out open spaces with scattered trees. Tropical kingbirds live at the edges of tropical forests, in woodlands, and along rivers or streams. They also live in savannas.

Tropical kingbirds sing a "dawn song," or a call heard before sunrise.

Like toco toucans, tropical kingbirds live in the upper branches of trees.

Tropical kingbirds depend on their habitat for food. Tropical kingbirds use the open space of their habitat to chase insects through the air. They mostly hunt for bees, beetles, butterflies, and moths. They also eat tropical fruit. At night, they sleep in the branches of trees.

# TOCO TOUCANS VS. ROCK WRENS

A rock wren pinches a low-flying insect in its pointy beak. Rock wrens live in dry, rocky habitats on cliffs and other high places. They seek out areas with mountains and plenty of rocks and boulders.

Rock wrens depend on their habitat for food and water. They eat spiders, insects, and larvae. Rock wrens find their prey under rocks, inside cracks in rocks, and in the shaded spaces between rocks. The food of the rock wren is also the bird's only source of water. That's because their habitat gets very little rain. Rock wrens are so used to getting water from their food that they don't drink water when they find it.

A rock wren feeds on an insect.

# COMPARE IT!

**TOCO TOUCANS**  VS.  **ROCK WRENS**

Open tropical areas with scattered trees  ◄ **HABITAT** ►  Dry, rocky areas at high elevations

**SOUTH AMERICA**  ◄ GEOGRAPHIC RANGE ►  **WESTERN CANADA, WESTERN UNITED STATES, AND CENTRAL AMERICA**

**STREAMS AND PONDS**  ◄ SOURCE OF WATER ►  **SPIDERS, INSECTS, AND LARVAE**

# CHAPTER 3

# TOCO TOUCANS IN ACTION

**A toco toucan reaches for a fig with its big beak.** The toucan tosses back its head and swallows the fruit whole. Toco toucans mostly feed on fruit. They also eat insects and the eggs of other birds.

Toco toucans forage for food by hopping from branch to branch or gliding from tree to tree. Their long bills can reach fruits in places that are hard to get to, like branches that are too thin to stand on. Toco toucans also eat fruit off the ground.

A toco toucan uses its long beak to reach for fruit.

Toco toucans often forage in small flocks. They fly from tree to tree in a single-file line. They make croaking and grunting sounds to communicate with one another. The sounds call attention to good sources of food. They also warn of predators. Toco toucan predators include jaguars and eagles. Snakes prey on toco toucan eggs. When a toucan spots a predator, the toucan hides deep inside the hole of a tree.

A toco toucan tosses its head back to eat a piece of fruit.

## DID YOU KNOW?

**Toco toucans are some of the noisiest birds of the forest. Their grunts and croaks can be heard from HALF A MILE (0.8 kilometers) away.**

# TOCO TOUCANS VS. CEDAR WAXWINGS

A cedar waxwing plucks a blue cedar berry from a thin branch and gulps it down. Cedar waxwings live in North and Central America. They eat fruit and also some insects. Like toco toucans, they travel from place to place to find ripe fruit. When one kind of fruit is no longer in season, both toco toucans and cedar waxwings fly to where another fruit has ripened.

Cedar waxwings eat mostly fruit, but they also fly over water to catch insects.

Cedar waxwings forage in a flock. Like toco toucans, they are noisy birds that use sound to communicate and warn of predators. Most predators of cedar waxwings are other birds, including hawks and merlins.

# TOCO TOUCANS VS. COMMON LOONS

A common loon swims in the shallow part of a lake, sticking its head underwater to search for food. Common loons are omnivores. They hunt fish and also eat plants. To capture prey, common loons dive underwater. They swim downward with their webbed feet and grab the prey in their bill.

Unlike toucans, common loons are strong long-distance fliers. They can fly up to 70 miles (113 km) per hour. Each year, they migrate north for the summer and south for the winter. In their winter habitat, male loons stake out a territory. To scare away other male loons, they make a yodeling sound and forcefully flap their wings.

Adult common loons have few predators. They defend their young against gulls, eagles, raccoons, weasels, and other animals. Common loons have been known to stab small predators with their beak.

The common loon is a strong swimmer that can also see well underwater.

# COMPARE IT!

**TOCO TOUCANS**

VS.

**COMMON LOONS**

**FRUIT, SOME INSECTS, AND BIRD EGGS**

◀ MAIN FOOD ▶

**FISH AND SOME PLANTS**

Forages for fruit in trees and on the ground

◀ FOOD-FINDING STRATEGY ▶ Catches prey in water

# JAGUARS, SNAKES, AND EAGLES

◀ PREDATORS ▶

# GULLS, EAGLES, RACCOONS, AND WEASELS

# CHAPTER 4

# THE LIFE CYCLE OF A TOCO TOUCAN

**The life cycle of toco toucans begins with a fruit toss.** A male and female toco toucan offer fruit to each other by tossing it into the other's mouth. This behavior sends the message that they are ready to mate.

Toco toucans are playful with their mates, and pairs often groom each other.

After mating, a female toco toucan lays two to four eggs. Her nest is a hole in a tree trunk. Both she and the male take turns incubating the eggs, which hatch after about two and a half weeks.

Toco toucan chicks are born without feathers. Their eyes are closed tight. They are blind and depend on their parents to bring them insects and fruit to eat. The chicks begin to grow a bill and feathers after three weeks. By eight weeks, they are able to leave the nest. The young birds take up to four years to become adults. Toco toucans live for about twenty years.

A young toco toucan in its nest

# TOCO TOUCANS VS. BARRED OWLS

A barred owl hoots loudly from a tree as night falls. Male and female barred owls attract each other with sound. First, the male calls out loudly to his female partner. Then the female responds with a higher-pitched call. This behavior signals that it's time to mate. They remain a pair as long as both owls live.

Barred owls use holes high in trees for their nests. A female barred owl lays two to five eggs. About a month later, the chicks are born with their eyes closed. Both parents feed their chicks. The young owls leave the nest after about six weeks, but they stay with their parents for a few more months. They are ready to mate after two years. Barred owls can live more than ten years in the wild.

A barred owl chick clutches a flying squirrel.

# COMPARE IT!

TOCO TOUCANS   VS.   BARRED OWLS

Tree hole   ◄ LOCATION OF NEST ►   Tree hole

YES   ◄ CHICKS BORN BLIND? ►   YES

ABOUT 20 YEARS   ◄ LIFE SPAN IN THE WILD ►   ABOUT 10 YEARS

# TOCO TOUCANS VS. SOCIABLE WEAVERS

A sociable weaver adds another twig to its giant nest. The sociable weaver's life cycle is different from the life cycle of a toco toucan. After mating with her partner, a female sociable weaver lays her eggs in a large nest. The nest is built and shared by up to one hundred sociable weaver families. The nest looks like a haystack in a tree. Inside are tunnels leading to many nesting areas.

The sociable weaver nests with hundreds of other birds.

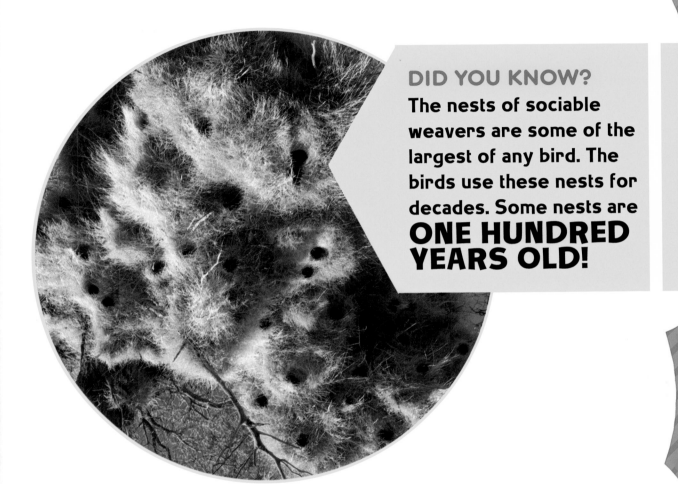

DID YOU KNOW?
The nests of sociable weavers are some of the largest of any bird. The birds use these nests for decades. Some nests are **ONE HUNDRED YEARS OLD!**

Male and female sociable weavers incubate their eggs in one of these nesting areas. The eggs hatch about two weeks later. The chicks are fed and cared for by their parents, brothers, and sisters. Even some neighboring sociable weavers might bring the chicks food. The chicks begin finding their own food after about two months. They are fully mature and ready to mate after two years. Sociable weavers live up to sixteen years.

# TOCO TOUCAN TRAIT CHART

This book explores toco toucans and the ways they are similar to and different from other birds. What other birds would you like to learn about?

| | WARM-BLOODED | FEATHERS ON BODY | LAYS HARD-SHELLED EGGS | HEAT-RELEASING BILL | NESTS IN TREE HOLES | EATS MOSTLY FRUIT |
|---|---|---|---|---|---|---|
| TOCO TOUCAN | X | X | X | X | X | X |
| KEEL-BILLED TOUCAN | X | X | X | X | X | X |
| NORTHERN BOBWHITE | X | X | X | | | |
| TROPICAL KINGBIRD | X | X | X | | | |
| ROCK WREN | X | X | X | | | |
| CEDAR WAXWING | X | X | X | | | X |
| COMMON LOON | X | X | X | | | |
| BARRED OWL | X | X | X | | X | |
| SOCIABLE WEAVER | X | X | X | | | |

**beak:** the jaws and mouth of a bird. Beaks are sometimes called bills, especially when they are long and flat.

**camouflages:** hides or disguises by covering up or changing the appearance of an animal

**communicate:** to transmit information to other animals using sound, sight, touch, taste, or smell

**flocks:** group of birds in a particular place that belong to one species

**forage:** to search for grass, fruit, and other plant parts to eat

**habitat:** an environment where an animal naturally lives. A habitat is where an animal can find food, water, air, and shelter, and raise its young.

**incubating:** sitting or standing over eggs to keep them warm. Eggs will not hatch if they are not kept at a safe temperature.

**larvae:** young wormlike forms (such as grubs or caterpillars) that hatch from the egg of many insects

**migrate:** to move from one area or habitat to another. Animals migrate to seek warmer or cooler climates or to find more plentiful prey.

**omnivores:** animals that eat both plants and meat

**predators:** animals that hunt, or prey on, other animals

**prey:** an animal that is hunted and killed by a predator for food

**roost:** to settle down to rest or sleep

**species:** animals that share common features and can produce offspring

**territory:** an area that is occupied and defended by an animal or a group of animals

**traits:** features that are inherited from parents. Body size and skin color are examples of inherited traits.

LERNER e SOURCE

Expand learning beyond the printed book. Download free, complementary educational resources for this book from our website, www.lerneresource.com.

# SELECTED BIBLIOGRAPHY

"Beak Design Absorbs High-Energy Impacts: Toco Toucan." *AskNature*. Accessed April 26, 2015. http://www.asknature.org/strategy/dabc8a57e2d063a6239d8648e337c109.

Behmke, Shannon. "*Ramphastos toco:* Toco Toucan."*Animal Diversity Web.* Accessed April 26, 2015. http://animaldiversity.org/accounts/Ramphastos_toco.

Sedgwick, Carolyn W. "*Ramphastos toco:* Toco Toucan." Cornell Lab of Ornithology. Accessed April 26, 2015. http://neotropical.birds.cornell.edu/portal/species/overview?p_p_spp=302936.

"Toco Toucan: *Ramphastos toco*." Phoenix Zoo. Accessed April 26, 2015. http://edventures.phoenixzoo.org/pdf/animalFactSheets/tocoToucan.pdf.

# FURTHER INFORMATION

Johnson, Jinny. *Animal Planet™ Atlas of Animals.* Minneapolis: Millbrook Press, 2012. Travel around the world and explore the planet's incredible animal diversity in this richly illustrated book.

*National Geographic:* Toucans http://animals.nationalgeographic.com/animals/birds/toucan Check out this *National Geographic* website for toucan facts and photos.

Ponka, Katherine. *Being a Toucan.* New York: Gareth Stevens, 2014. Imagine being a toucan searching for food, sleeping in a tree, and wrestling with other toucans.

The San Diego Zoo: Toucans http://animals.sandiegozoo.org/animals/toucan Learn interesting facts about toucans at the San Diego Zoo's website.

# INDEX

appearance, 6–7, 11

barred owl, 26–27

cedar waxwing, 20–21
common loon, 22–23

diet, 13, 18, 23

foraging, 18–19

habitat, 4, 12–15, 17

keel-billed toucan, 8–9

life cycle, 24–25, 26

northern bobwhite, 10–11

rock wren, 16–17

sociable weaver, 28–29
South America, 12

tropical kingbird, 14–15